CHANGING ATTITUDES
ABOUT DISABILITY

CHANGING ATTITUDES ABOUT DISABILITY

How to See People with Disabilities
as our Co-laborers in God's
Redemption Plan

Dan Vander Plaats

Dordt Press

Printed in the United States of America.

Dordt Press   www.dordt.edu/DCPcatalog
700 7th Street NE
Sioux Center, Iowa 51250

ISBN: 978-1-940567-23-5

The Library of Congress Cataloging-in-Publication Data is on file with the Library of Congress, Washington, D.C.

Library of Congress Control Number: 2020933291

This is a joint publication of Dordt Press, Disability Matters and Elim Christian Services, written by Dan Vander Plaats, Director of Advancement at Elim Christian Services. *The 5 Stages of Disability Attitudes* © 2009 is also by Dan Vander Plaats.

About Disability Matters

Disability Matters is a consortium of individuals with a passion to see God's people include those who have disabilities in our churches and communities. Founded by blogger Ellen Stumbo (http://www.ellenstumbo.com), the site provides resources, blogs, and network connections that seek to advance the inclusion of people with disabilities.

About Elim

At Elim—www.elimsc.org—we know that everyone is "created in Christ Jesus to do good works" (Ephesians 2:10). Our mission is to "equip individuals with disabilities to pursue their God-given potential." To do this, we provide person-centered services on two Chicago-area campuses, and we provide networking, consulting, and professional training services to other schools and organizations to help them become places where, as we articulate in our vision: *people with disabilities thriving in their communities.*

Elim is a special place that continues to be shaped by the following core values:

- We are Christ-centered
- We all have value and purpose
- We are a learning and sharing community

Elim is both the inspiration for and the continuing steward of "The 5 Stages" and has provided all its relevant resources, including a website, blog, and several translations.

CONTENT

the 5 stages
changing attitudes

A RESOURCE OF ELIM CHRISTIAN SERVICES

STAGE 1: IGNORANCE

Weaknesses and disabilities are a sign that God either does not care or is not able to fix the situation. In fact, they may be a result of sin or a lack of faith. God is not involved in the life of someone with a disability, because He can't use people who are so broken. I do not know people with disabilities, nor do I know anything about disabilities. I have no interest in getting to know them or to know more about their life.

STAGE 2: PITY

I feel sorry for people with disabilities. It's too bad, really. I am blessed by God and I can help others. I am grateful that my children are not disabled. People with weaknesses and disabilities obviously need someone like me to help them and give them meaning, due to their troubles. I really don't see any meaning or purpose to their lives.

STAGE 3: CARE

Like me, people with disabilities were created in God's image. By that virtue alone they have value. I hope that someone will take the time to show them God's love, and I will happily support such an effort. In fact, I think we need to find ways to help those people. Maybe we should start a special church education class, or respite care for the sake of the parents.

STAGE 4: FRIENDSHIP

I have come to know and spend time with a friend who has a disability. This person has value in God's sight, but also in mine, and I know that my life is better for having known this person, and as much as I have helped her, she has also blessed me. In fact, I now like to initiate relationships with people who have disabilities. God brings many different people into my church and community, including people with disabilities, and we all benefit as we grow in friendship with each other.

STAGE 5: CO-LABORERS

If God has called each of us to serve and praise Him with every fiber of our beings, then He has done the same for our brothers and sisters in Christ with disabilities. I think ministry should not just be to people with disabilities, but with or alongside people who have disabilities. Together, we will encourage and equip each other, with and without disabilities, into every good work to respond to God's call on our lives. We can all give and we can all receive.

AWARENESS ▸ ACCESS ▸ INTEGRATION ▸ ENGAGEMENT

THE 5 STAGES: CHANGING ATTITUDES" ©COPYRIGHT ©2009 DAN VANDER PLAATS
WITH THANKS TO ELIM CHRISTIAN SERVICES, DISABILITY CONCERNS CRC
DISABILITY CONCERNS RCA, JONI AND FRIENDS, AND MANY OTHERS

SCAN THIS CODE OR GO TO
WWW.THE5STAGES.COM FOR MORE
INFORMATION AND RESOURCES.

Introduction

Several years ago, my husband sent me a link to *The 5 Stages of Disability Attitudes*. I run Disability Matters, an organization with the mission to encourage every church to embrace disability, and the vision to see disability as an organic part of every church. "I think you need to share *The 5 Stages* with every church you help," he said.

It did not take me long to recognize that my husband was right. He was a pastor at the time, and he felt that during his schooling he was never truly prepared to include people with disabilities at church. *The 5 Stages* is, in my opinion, the best tool available to get conversation started, and to challenge our own views on disability.

When I speak at churches and conferences and participate in Disability Awareness Sundays, I always teach on *The 5 Stages*. If we want people to understand how people with disabilities are invaluable members of the Body of Christ, if we want to see Luke 14 in action, we must understand what it means to be co-laborers.

This outstanding book provides the background to why Dan created *The 5 Stages*, and really delves into each stage in ways that make it personal and practical.

Ellen Stumbo
Founder and Director of Disability Matters
www.whydisabilitymatters.org

Prologue

I hope you don't care about people with disabilities.

No, I mean that. I am hoping you don't actually think about, prioritize, spend time with, or know anyone with a disability. Because if you don't care, then you are exactly who I am hoping will seriously consider what follows.

This book(let) is for the person who doesn't care: the guy who has never even met someone with a disability, the woman who worries that the autistic kid in her child's class might somehow have a negative impact on her child, the neighbor who doesn't get beyond looking out the window …wondering.

This book is for people who don't care about people with disabilities and who could stand to change their attitude.

But, why would you want to do that?

What if I told you that your church would be better for everyone if it included people with disabilities? What if making your business more accessible could actually improve your profits? What if adding children with special needs to your child's classroom could improve your kid's grades?

Maybe that hits home for you. But maybe there is an even more important reason to change your attitude.

Maybe you should change your attitude simply because God created you, and he created me. He calls us both to serve him, to glorify him, to use our gifts and talents in service to his kingdom.

All that is true of both of us, even though *I have a disability*.

I talk funny, and yet God still has the same calling on me that he does on you. He has gifted me and my other friends with disabilities as generously as he has gifted you.

You might not care right now, but I hope you can see why that disbelieving attitude should change. And by the end of this book, I think you'll wonder why you haven't changed your point of view already.

It's time for people with disabilities to belong in your church, in your school and business, and in your life. Not because we deserve it, or because we're just as important as you, but because of God.

He called us to encourage one another, and build each other up (1 Thessalonians), to make disciples (Matthew 28). And he didn't add an asterisk or caveat to those commands.

He doesn't exempt anyone from his call, from doing the good works that were prepared in advance for each of us to do (Ephesians 2). Every person is created in God's image, with a purpose in his kingdom, with value to his church, and without exception. There is no asterisk attached to God's call, one that says, "except for people with disabilities."

> *For we are God's handiwork, created in Christ Jesus to do good works, which God prepared in advance for us to do.* Ephesians 2:10

People with disabilities are supposed to be part of our missional communities, our churches.

Why?

Because there is no asterisk.

Disabled and Not Disabled

I don't remember being picked on as a student at Orange City Christian School in Northwest Iowa. That's maybe the thing that stands out most for me, considering I do have a funny-sounding voice. I would expect that more people would have picked on me. In fact, not only did other students not pick on me, they actively prevented others from picking on me.

Everyone did. Even the boy who was tall, confident, and athletic. We had nothing in common. Except for *Star Wars*. He loved it, and so did I. We talked about it, talked about and played with our favorite action figures, and he reveled in sharing news about the upcoming movies with me.

I am Disabled

One time, I was over at his house and I don't even remember what we were doing, but his neighbor friend came over to play. Not very self-aware, I said hi and we talked about what we could play. This other boy asked my friend why I talked funny. I remember that.

I remember how it felt. I remember looking down at my playing hands and realizing something was wrong with me. My parents had told me before, but I never really heard it in my own voice. Even today, to my own ears, I sound perfectly normal, unless I really work to listen and hear the weird noises that come out.

But I also remember my friend almost spitting back at this boy, "He doesn't talk funny." I remember my friend's mom coming out on the stoop to sternly talk to this boy for saying that. I remember feeling a little bad for the boy, but feeling very good about me.

I remember that as the first time I got picked on. I remember how my friend and his mom didn't even hesitate to stand up for me and be my friends. My real friends. And I remember it as the first time I asked why God did this to me.

I am not Disabled

My friend and his mom would not allow this young boy to make me feel different, to make me feel lesser, because of my disability.

In fact, my parents and friends had done much to make sure my expectations in life were in no way diminished by the reality of disability, sometimes even unintentionally.

Because they saw me as "normal," I mostly saw myself as normal too. That's why I, like many others, have been so uncomfortable around people who have disabilities. I didn't see how they fit into my world, nor why they should be part of it.

When I was little, my mom worked as a nurse at a place called Hope Haven, in Northwest Iowa. Hope Haven was home to many adults with disabilities, and I felt very uncomfortable on the one occasion that I remember visiting her workplace.

On a school field trip to nearby Sioux Falls, we visited a "school for the deaf" and enjoyed a dramatic performance by some of their students. But once again, I didn't want to be around that place.

I did not like people with disabilities. I talked about it one time with my mom, telling her how uncomfortable those people made me feel. "Well, just remember," she cajoled. "You are disabled too, you know."

Okay. Fine. I am disabled.

The words stung, even when I was barely a teenager. You are disabled. I remember thinking even then that I had a bad attitude toward people who had disabilities, and feeling doubly bad because I was one such myself.

My mom was just reminding me of the importance of our disability attitudes. Our attitudes toward people who have disabilities says a great deal about how we view God, and what we believe he sees in us. Our disability attitudes aren't just a disability issue. They are a discipleship issue.

If we believe in the God that is proclaimed in the Bible, we will accept that our attitudes toward people with disabilities must change. The next several chapters will assist you in doing just that.

So, stick with me, because we're just getting started.

Questions to Consider
- o   When have you been made to feel like you were different or didn't fit in?
- o   Are differences important, and why?
- o   What does the Bible teach us about our differences?

Why *The 5 Stages* Exists

I am disabled in that I have a pretty obvious speech impediment. But I am not disabled in the way that most people think of someone with disabilities. I can do most anything that a "normal" person can do; my mind works pretty much the standard way. So, I guess you could say I am not really disabled.

I see myself that way too, in my everyday moments anyway. I don't generally look at myself and think, "I'm disabled." Then again, does anybody who's disabled do that?

Because I don't see myself as disabled, I have always had a hard time identifying with people who have disabilities. I think most of that comes from not wanting to see myself that way, even when I'm facing that reality head-on.

Staring Disability in the Face

Several years ago, I was at a big concert venue where we were promoting Elim and our programs, and we were a long way from home. I was there with two other Elim staff members, two Elim adult clients, Stacey and Christina, and a good friend from Food for the Hungry.

We were all exhausted at the end of the day, so we ducked into the air-conditioned steakhouse a few blocks from our hotel to get some food. When our waitress got to the table, her bubbly personality made us all smile. She asked us all our names, and when Stacey and Christina spoke, she noticed they had some impairments, so her tone of voice changed. Her voice went a little higher, her head cocked to the side a little bit, and she spoke even more kindly—if a little condescendingly—to my friends from Elim.

I thought that was great. She was trying so hard to engage them and speak to them. She was such a nice young lady.

Until she turned to me. When I said hi, she noticed my speech impediment. Right away she noticed. And I've tried to hide it before, so I can tell when I've fooled someone into thinking I don't have a speech impediment. I didn't fool her.

And then—from my perspective, at least—she went from being a kind and sweet young lady to an awful, rude, ignorant person, all because she started talking to and treating me the same way she treated Christina and Stacey. How terribly rude.

But I'm not as Disabled as Them

It bothered me until I got back to my hotel room that night.

I didn't really understand what it was that bothered me. I called my wife to tell her about it and talk it through. This event had troubled me, and I couldn't put my finger on the problem.

Finally, it clicked. I realized that what upset me was not that I was treated in such a way, but that I had no problem with that nice young lady's attitude until it was directed at me.

But that Doesn't Make Me More Valuable

Why was it okay for her to talk down to my friends, but not to me? What made me "more worthy" of simple common courtesy and respect?

More than that, I thought about how our adults and kids get treated at Elim. I knew our teachers, support staff, instructors, and supervisors were never condescending, no matter how disabled a student or adult was. In fact, if anything, our team was almost "mean" by comparison, always keeping high expectations of the students, calling out inappropriate behaviors in adults, holding each other to account in a way that said, "As a child of God, you are expected to act, talk, and work in a certain way. I am not lowering my expectations of you just because you are having a bad day or because you have this or that disability. I respect you too much to condescend to you."

My coworkers at Elim had always acted this way, and I had learned some of that behavior from them. But this was all new to me.

It was that night that I started to map out *The 5 Stages of Disability Attitudes*. And in the next chapter I'll share the biblical foundations that form the foundation of *The 5 Stages*.

Questions to Consider

- o In the meantime, can you share a time when you felt like you were unfairly judged as "lacking" in some way? How did that make you feel?
- o What is a God-honoring way of looking at people with disabilities?

The Foundations of *The 5 Stages*

The 5 Stages seek to convince you, and to enable you to convince others, that life lived alongside people who have disabilities is not optional. It is essential to our lives as followers of Christ.

But these arguments do not hold in and of themselves. They connect because they are supported by a strong, biblical foundation. These foundations include:

- **Disability is not a blessing and it is also not a curse.** People made in the image of their Creator are blessings, disabilities are not. Yet a disability is also not a curse. Jesus tells us this very directly in John 9. The disciples asked Jesus why a man was born blind, assuming it was due to some kind of sin. Jesus tells them simply that neither this man nor his parents sinned. It's not a curse. Yet we also know, from living life with a disability, that it is not a blessing. It is not always easy; and it rarely makes one's life more enjoyable than it would be without the disability.

- **We are all disabled and we are all also not disabled.** We are all broken, and all have sinned and fallen short of God's glory (Romans 3). So yes, we all have disabilities and shortcomings. But your slight case of debility is not the same as complete blindness or a crippling mental illness. Your pre-dilections and sinful desires are an impediment to living a life that glorifies God, but they are not the same as someone's inability to walk or to feed themselves. More notably, you saying that we are the same is often just an effort to absolve your-self of any obligation to come to our aid, to put yourself out on our behalf. We may all have some special area of disability, but some of us need ex-tra help, and that is just a reality of life.

- **Our value does not come from accomplish-ment or from being disabled, but only from God.** Our intrinsic worth is not based on extrin-sic value systems that celebrate accomplishments like graduation, athletic prowess, or employabil-ity. Neither does our value come from peculiar qualities that make us "unique." Rather, the sum total of our value is defined and seen only in re-lation to our Creator. (See Matthew 10:31, Ro-mans 5:8, and many other verses, to understand our value in God's sight.)

- **God made me, but I don't know that he made me this way.** We have record of God doing things to harden people's hearts, to make them lame, but we also know he is our God who uses terrible things and situations to redeem his world and ac-complish his purposes. He only does good. Say-ing he made me this way can easily lead to concluding that everything about being disabled is just fine. When it isn't. We know that God makes us each to be who we are (Psalm 139), but I just can't say for sure that he makes us *the way* we are. So, did God create me? Yes. Did he intend my disability, or did he just allow it? I don't know.

Each of these foundations is important to confront and accept in order to really grasp the meaning of each of *The 5 Stages*. Disability is a part of life, and people who have disabilities are his children, the same as you. Each person is a masterpiece of their Creator, created to do the good works that were prepared in advance for each one to do.

Questions to Consider

- o What do you think? Are people with disabilities more important, more loving, and godlier than people who do not have disabilities?
- o What has drawn you into a relationship with someone who is disabled?

I've been bullied my whole entire life.

When I was three years old, I was diagnosed with Attention Deficit Disorder, and then by five years old I had nine ear infections. I couldn't hear. My mom and my dad and my sister thought that I was going to be deaf, that I had to go to the doctor and get tubes in my ears.

People would tease me, and make fun of me, and tell me that I'm retarded. When they told me that I was retarded, it made me feel like: I could do anything. But they don't *think I could do anything. People still tease me, but not as much they did when I was coming to grips with these realities when I was in school.*

They don't understand what I go through. They've never been there before. They don't know what I have gone through when I was growing up, and when people teased me when I was growing up. It just hurt.

They would call me "four-eyes," or they would say that I'm ugly, or that I'm not cute.

As a person, I am no different than everybody else, but everybody else doesn't see it that way. I am a person just like you. I have a disability.

But they don't understand that, so then I have to explain it to them.

I don't feel that ignorance any more.

Stacey

Co-laborer
Elim Christian Services

Stage 1: Ignorance

You walk into a restaurant for a Saturday evening meal and notice that there's an open table. As the hostess escorts you to the table, you notice a young man at a neighboring table making a scene, incessantly making small hopping movements in his chair and occasionally rocking back and forth. You have no idea what might be prompting this person to do this, and you really don't want to know. You simply ask the hostess to find another table.

You are just leaving Sunday worship services when another member comes up to you and tells you about a wonderful seminar they just attended where everyone was encouraged to assess their church building's accessibility. They wonder if you'd help. "What for?" you reply. "There are no disabled people here anyway."

You are annoyed. You pull into a parking lot, see a great spot open right near the door and then, halfway in, you see the sign saying, "Handicapped Parking Only." Why do they even have all these spots, you say to yourself. It's not like there's that many people—and the people using those spots are probably just abusing the system, like always!

How are all of these examples of ignorance? Some folks might seem a tad insensitive, but ignorant?

What is Ignorance?

Ignorance is "being blind" to an issue or a concept. It

is being uninformed, unaware, or disconnected. Ignorance is largely unintentional, and yet it is so simple to move past ignorance that it can appear intentional when people stay there.

Ignorance is also a necessary first step in any journey. Before we can make any progress in anything, we must first get past the point where we have no understanding of it.

So, ignorance is necessary. There must always be a point where you are ignorant.

But hopefully, not for long.

Ignorance is a negative word for a good reason. No one who finds out that they're ignorant about something wants to stay that way, or to have others realize that they are, in fact, ignorant.

What Keeps us Ignorant?

When we live life apart from people with disabilities, doing so can connect us to some troubling ways of thinking: We can think that people with disabilities are in their condition because of some sin of theirs or their parents. Remember the disciples in John 9 ("Rabbi, who sinned, this man or his parents?").

This way of thinking is troubling and reflects the very same ignorance displayed by the Lord's disciples.

We can think that people with disabilities cannot be used by God. I thought this myself. My most fervent request of God was that he remove my speech impediment …this one little thing that kept me from being normal. I believed that being "normal" was the only way in which

God could really use me.

We can think, inversely, that life without disability (or difficulty) is a reflection of God's blessing. We who seek to serve God wonder why he would allow us to experience difficulty after we have devoted ourselves to his service. Yet God clearly tells us that those who seek to serve the Lord will suffer (or be persecuted—see 2 Timothy 3:12).

These ways of thinking inform our actions. They prompt us to keep our distance. They compel us to keep apart from others, and they are dynamic in that these ignorant assumptions are *actively dividing the family of God.* They keep us from enjoying the full communion of his kingdom.

How Can I Move Beyond Ignorance?

Pray

- Pray that God might open your eyes to the prevalence of people with disabilities.
- Pray that you might have the opportunity to connect with someone who lives with a disability.
- Pray that God might give you a heart of grace and mercy toward those who are different.

Reflect

- If 19 percent of the world's population is living with some kind of disability, why am I not connected to anyone who lives with a disability?
- In what ways have I ignored, been annoyed by, or do I lack empathy for people who live with

disabilities?

- What conclusions do I jump to about people with disabilities? What role do I believe sin plays in the lives of people with disabilities?
- What do I assume about the value of people with disabilities?
- Does God have a purpose and plan for their lives?

Act

- Seek to be introduced to someone who has a disability. Don't pursue this as an opportunity to "have a disabled friend." Instead, please view this as an opportunity to simply establish a connection with a brother or sister in Christ. See others first as people, and second as people with differences.
- Read Mark 10 and Matthew 20. In both passages, we hear slightly different accounts of what appears to be the same story, in which Jesus restores sight to someone who is blind. In each story, the crowd rebukes the blind man to "be quiet." After you read this story, think about the ways you and your congregation have rebuked and ignored people who live with disabilities.
- Ask one other person (or, even better, ask your family) if they knew that 17 percent of their neighbors are living with some kind of disability. Ask them who they know who lives with a disability.

Questions to Consider

- ○ What is your attitude toward people with disabilities?
- ○ Can you remember the last time you treated someone with disabilities out of an attitude of ignorance?
- ○ What leads you to believe that people with disabilities have no place in your life?

Resources

Here are some other resources that can help you move beyond ignorance:

- *Dancing with Max: A mother and a son who broke free* (Grand Rapids MI: Zondervan, 2010 – ISBN 978-0310000198), a book by Emily Colson—with a Foreword and Epilogue by Max's grandfather, Chuck Colson—in which she shares life with her son Max, who has autism.
- *Sun Shine Down: Memoir* (Ossining NY: T.S. Poetry Press, 2013 – ISBN 0989854207), by Gillian Marchenko. Gillian shares not only the challenges of life after giving birth to a daughter who has Down syndrome, but also shares a very raw account of her own personal challenges from that moment forward.
- Check out *The Irresistible Church*, a blog and resource website (irresistiblechurch.org) put together by Joni and Friends. This site will introduce you to what a welcoming church really looks like.

Pity means when you feel sorry for someone like in a wheelchair. You feel compassionate for that person.

A lot of times when you are in a restaurant, and you get ignored, you get shoved in a corner, because they think I'm more different than they are.

I feel angry but I always felt different.

Bob

Co-laborer
Elim Christian Services

Stage 2: Pity

Over the last twenty years, I have guided thousands of visitors on tours of Elim's ministry headquarters and have shared with them the resources we provide to people with disabilities. On all those tours, there is always someone who is stuck. They are in a viewpoint rut and they can't get out.

They look around the Elim community, and all they see is reason to despair, to feel sorry and hopeless, to wish that God would either heal them—those people with disabilities—or take them home to heaven for eternal healing.

I can understand how they get stuck in that mindset. I get in that same rut myself sometimes.

The viewpoint they're stuck on is what I call "pity," the second stage on the journey of disability attitudes. Pity is a necessary and important step in the disability attitudes' journey. In fact, pity—as negative as I make it sound—is a good thing. God commands us to show pity to those in need.

> *He will take pity on the weak and the needy*
> *and save the needy from death.* Psalm 72:13

Not only does the Bible teach us to show pity, there is also a sound reason to do so. Where there is a real weakness, or deficiency, or frailty—as with poverty, broken relationships, and illness—we must take extra care. And let's not be so misguided as to think that disability does not include weakness. It most certainly does.

If the Bible calls us to show pity to those who experience weakness or suffering, and we accept that people who have disabilities have weaknesses, then pity is a necessary and important step in the journey of disability attitudes.

Don't get Stuck in Negative Pity

But there is a problem with pity. It is very easy to get stuck there.

Pity feeds on itself. Whether you feel sorry for others or for yourself, it is often because you see no other way around it, except to feel pity.

While pity is necessary, it is too often negative. It is a way of keeping our distance from people with disabilities. In fact, it often seems as though negative pity is the only thing that keeps us from progressing in the journey of disability attitudes.

So, what is negative pity?

Negative pity convinces us of one thing over and over again: "It's just too bad." And you keep thinking it and saying it whenever you see someone in a wheelchair, or struggling with behaviors, or unable to see what is happening around them. It's just too bad.

It's just too bad…. It's just too bad.

It's Not Just Too Bad

And it is too bad. It's not good that we have disabilities. It is not good to lack the ability to walk or run. It is not a good thing to be sightless when there are so many wonderful things to see; to be unable to communicate in a world that is rife with images and symbols and words that enrich our lives, by God's grace.

But it is more than just too bad. Unfortunately, negative pity never stops saying "It's just too bad."

But positive pity adds four words and a question mark: *What can I do?*

Isn't that amazing? It can be (and in many ways is) that simple. The difference between negative and positive pity is four words and a question mark. What can I do?

What can I do to help? What can I do to assist you in getting to your seat? What can I do to make sure you can communicate? What can I do?

It's so simple, and it gets us so far! The movement from negative pity to positive pity makes a world of difference for many people. The inability to move beyond Stage 2 is entirely wrapped up in the issue of negative pity.

How can You Add Four Words and a Question Mark?

We know that pity is necessary. For that matter, it is also important. It is not simple to live life with a disability. Those challenges will sometimes invite an attitude of pity. While pity is necessary, it does contain both a positive and a negative quality. So, what can you do to foster positive pity, and even move beyond it?

Pray

- Pray that God would show you how your pity keeps you "apart from" people who live with disabilities.

- Pray for a spirit of openness to talk to a person who lives with disabilities, and to simply ask them about their day.

Reflect

- Why is "That's too bad!" so often the extent of my response to the challenges others face?
- How does negative pity keep me from getting to know people who live with disabilities?
- Are people with disabilities less valuable to God?

Act

- Read Luke 14:1–23. In both his discussion with the pharisees and in his parable of the great banquet, what is Jesus telling us about people who live with disabilities? What is he saying about their place in the kingdom of God, if indeed they have one?
- Discuss the fact that people who live with disabilities are twice as likely to be unemployed and are 2½ times more likely to live in poverty. Ask how this kind of injustice can be fixed.

Questions to Consider

- In what ways have you expressed negative pity about someone you perceive to have a more difficult life?
- What is your attitude about that person's potential or capability? Share your thoughts in the comments section below.

Resources

And finally, here are some more resources that can help you learn to ask: "What can I do?"

- Read through the diagram (or one of the translations) provided as a resource by Elim Christian Services: *The 5 Stages: Changing Attitudes* (www. the 5stages.com).

- Read the very short but very eye-opening *From Brokenness to Community* (Mahwah NJ: Paulist Press, 1992 – ISBN 978-0809133413), by Jean Vanier.

- Get a glimpse of how a Catholic priest was deeply changed by life with someone who had disabilities in *In the Name of Jesus: Reflections on Christian leadership* (Chestnut Ridge NY: Crossroad Publishing: 1989 – ISBN 978-0824512590), by Henri J.M. Nouwen.

A good kind of compassion to me is like if, say, I was in my wheelchair and I had to go somewhere fast. Now I know I can't push myself that fast, so if I ask somebody to push me fast and they do it.

I'm training for the Special Olympics, which are in May, and my friend has agreed to help me in walking around the track. My friend has shown care by just grabbing my hand and walking me along the track.

I show compassion by every month going to Daybreak Homeless Shelter [in Joliet, Illinois] and making the food for the homeless and then serving it to them.

It makes me feel really good to know I am changing somebody's life because they count on me.

Jennifer

Co-laborer
Elim Christian Services

Stage 3: Care

When we started this journey, we were ignorant of people who lived with disabilities. Then we learned about positive and negative pity. These are two necessary steps in the journey, but I think it's safe to say that here is where the real work begins. It also happens to be where we finally start to reflect God's kingdom in our thoughts and attitudes.

The third stage of disability attitudes is CARE, which *The 5 Stages* diagram explains as follows:

"Like me, people with disabilities were created in God's image. By that virtue alone they have value. I hope that someone will take the time to show them God's love, and I will happily support such an effort. In fact, I think we need to find ways to help those people. Maybe we should start a special church education class, or respite care for the sake of the parents."

Care reflects God's heart for people with disabilities by:

- acknowledging their presence in our lives and communities.
- recognizing the need for assistance.
- seeking to meet their needs and provide them with opportunities to learn and achieve.

What does Caring Look Like?

An attitude of Care was behind the building of Elim Christian Services (www.elimcs.org), and it also built many other ministries. When people supported Joni Eareckson Tada, she and her family built Joni and Friends (www.joniandfriends.org). When a large community of Lutherans saw the needs of families with disabilities, they began building Bethesda (bethesdalc.org) in Wisconsin. These groups of people responded with care because they saw something that others didn't.

They looked beyond incapacity. They saw past the issue of brokenness and difference. They saw fellow children of God. They understood that we are each made in his image. We each have different abilities and weaknesses. Yet we each are made to reflect his image.

Caring is good, so good, in fact, that we believe taking care of those who have disabilities is all we need to do. We stop our journey through the disability attitudes because we mistakenly believe we have reached our destination.

Why Caring is Not Enough

But why, you might ask, is it so bad to stop at caring?

- **Because there is no relationship**. There is no reciprocity. The thinking of someone who stops at Care can be summed up as "Because you need help, and I don't, we are in different social classes. You can associate with your kind, and I'll associate with mine." That kind of stings, doesn't it? When there is no relationship, it is because at least one party has no use for the other party. I can help you, but you have nothing to offer me, so why should we spend any time together?

- **Because there is no accountability**. Where there is no relationship, there can be no accountability. Accountability is needed because we all have vices, we all struggle, we all slide down to the minimum expectation. I know this because I see the reverse at play every single day at Elim. Because our teachers, paraprofessionals, case managers, and supervisors know the people we serve, they call each person to account for their behavior, for their effort, for their hearts and attitudes.

- **Because there is no opportunity**. When we stop at Care, we keep people with disabilities from opportunities to achieve whatever God has called them to do. We assume, somehow, that they have nothing to offer, not just to us, and not just to the church or the community, but to God himself.

How Can I Move Beyond Caring?

Caring is great. It is essential! But it is also just a step on the journey. It is not the final step, not by a long shot. It is only halfway through the journey of disability attitudes. How can this be? What is it that makes us think that simply caring for people is the highest possible attitude we could adopt? How can we move beyond it?

Pray

- Pray for a spirit of vulnerability, that you might

become open to a deeper relationship with someone who lives with disabilities.

- Pray that God would show you what his kingdom looks like when each person is valued as God sees them, and not as we see each other.

Reflect

- Why do I believe that "caring" is the highest and best attitude to have towards someone with disabilities?

- Read 1 Samuel 16. In it, Samuel is reproached by God for overlooking David, because: "People look at the outward appearance, but the LORD looks at the heart." How does this tendency lead me to the idea that I am only called to care, and no more?

- Why do people with disabilities who visit my church have to sit in one section of the church? What does that mean for my brothers and sisters in Christ who have autism or other disorders? Are they not welcome before the throne?

Act

- If your congregation offers a disability ministry of some kind, offer your assistance. Make snacks, help with one of the participants.

- If your church does not offer a disability ministry, ask your elders or deacons why. Ask some of your friends and fellow church members why. Offer to host a coffee where you and your fellow church members can talk more about this opportunity.

- Take extra time to assist people with disabilities with whom you come into contact, whether it's offering to open a door if needed, or being patient in listening to the thoughts, concerns, and joys of someone who has difficulty communicating.
- Support a ministry that provides services to individuals with disabilities, like an children's educational program, or an adult day program.
- Discuss the reality that over 50 percent of families with people with disabilities do not attend church regularly because they do not feel welcome.

Questions to Consider
- In what ways do you show your care and compassion for people who have disabilities?
- Why do we so often stop at care? Why do we think that that is the most we need to do?

Resources
- Connect to the website for Disability Matters (whydisabilitymatters.org), an online community founded by Ellen Stumbo.
- Get a solid theological understanding about how we view disability by reading the excellent *Same Lake, Different Boat: Coming alongside people touched by disability* (Phillipsburg NJ: P&R Publishing, 2006 – ISBN 978-1596380516), by Stephanie Hubach.

- Henri J.M. Nouwen shares a deeply moving account of the days he spent with his friend in his last book, *Adam: God's Beloved* (Maryknoll NY: Orbis Books, 1997 – ISBN 978-1570759949).

Did God Make Me This Way?

I was born with a disability. I have never liked the disability, but it is part of my everyday life. It seems like it's a part of me, and that I wouldn't be the same person if I didn't have a speech impediment.

The mother of a child with Down syndrome or autism probably doesn't like the social, behavioral, and medical issues that accompany the "disability." And yet, there is a freshness in her child's perspective, a different take on the world that is both unique and somehow essential. In some mysterious way, God's wonders are revealed in the life of this person.

These wonders—God's patience, his stillness, his ability to look at the heart instead of what man usually looks at, and his strength in weakness—seem so important to understand that we reasonably conclude that God wanted us to learn them. And if he wanted us to learn them, perhaps he *needed* to send that child, with their disabilities and struggles and all. And that begs the question I try to respond to here. Did God make me this way?

Did God make me with a disability, and, if so, why? If he made me this way, what does that mean for my value, what does it mean for my place in God's kingdom? What does it mean for people with disabilities?

If God Made Me This Way…

I want to say that God did make me this way, because:

- it means that God is sovereign, which is what I've been taught. It's what the Bible proclaims.
- it means that I am still okay just the way I am, because "God doesn't make junk and he doesn't junk what he has made," and
- it means that my disability is actually okay (just a "difference" or a "different ability"), if not actually a really good blessing from God.

I want to believe that God made me this way because it is affirming, and it would seem consistent with my perception of what it means for God to be "loving." If God is all these things (a powerful God who is sovereign and "works all things together for our good"—Romans 8:28), then it is easiest to accept disability as some kind of intentional gift from God, and, therefore, good.

After all, some persons with autism believe their ability to approach a problem from a different perspective is a talent, and not at all a deficit. Parents of children with Down syndrome appreciate their child's different attitude on life. In short, some very real and unique gifts are evident in the lives of people with disabilities. And the presence of those gifts can make disability appear to be a very good gift indeed.

But I Know It's Not A Gift…

Just as I know disability is not just a curse, as has been

thought for so long, I also know it is not a gift. The idea of it being a blessing is a more recent development, for all the reasons I listed above, plus a more fundamental one.

We want to believe that there's nothing fundamentally wrong with us.

Being disabled is not a moral "wrong." It is not the same as being inclined to lie, cheat, and steal—these are all sinful defects of the human condition.

But there are other "symptoms" of the human condition that are not inherently sinful, but still speak to the broken nature of our world. As tough as it can be to accept, it seems like disability is one of those symptoms.

Being disabled is a real-world sign that things are not the way they are supposed to be, that the kingdom of this world is broken. All Creation has been affected by the Fall, in all aspects, and this is true not only in our moral lives, but in our spiritual, physical, intellectual, emotional, and psychological lives as well.

Disability is not the same as sinful desires. There is nothing that needs to be "fixed" for people with disabilities to serve God. However, even though they don't need to be fixed, that does not mean that there is nothing deficient or wrong about disability.

Instead, we realize that the God's purpose in disability is _not_ some object lesson in morality or faith, or the lack thereof. It is instead a means by which God can and does reveal himself to the world. He speaks through disability. His presence is simultaneously, equally, and fully revealed and accessible in the lives of an adult man with autism, in an infant with cerebral palsy, as much as it is revealed through a "gifted" leader or an "accomplished" worker.

God reveals his love for us through disability. He speaks to us about how much he values us through the lives of people with disabilities. He reminds us how he moves, sometimes quickly, and sometimes slowly, through the presence of people with disabilities. This doesn't make disability good, nor does it make it bad. But God does his good through it.

Is Ability a Gift, or is it a Curse?

Our temptation is to see disability as a curse or as a gift because of what disability means within different contexts. The same is true for "ability." We assume that a deficiency in ability is a problem, and conversely that ability is a gift.

But is it truly a gift? If we are able on our own to achieve success and accomplish tasks, then at some point we could reasonably question the need for God. Is it possible that our "ability" is actually a curse?

Consider the rich young ruler—surely, he was gifted that he was able to accumulate such wealth, to be blessed by God with his resources. Yet it is his very dependence on that wealth, on what we perceive as a gift from God, that prevents him from following God. His gifts draw him away from God, to exchange the truth of God for the lies of wealth.

The puzzle that confronts us in this reality is that sin's existence is somehow necessary to God's redemptive story and is therefore part of our own stories. His plan mysteriously requires its presence and is perfected in its defeat.

Additionally, God in his wisdom designed us to be perfected through his suffering, through the sacrifice and resurrection of his Son. He has also called us to individual journeys that are written most fully only through our own pain and suffering.[1]

We are made into his perfect creations in part by difficulty and disappointment, by challenges and constant chafing, even by hurt and by hate.

So, ability is not necessarily the clear "gift" we often consider it to be. Yet, this is not a reason to consider it a curse, either. Truly, God grants us gifts and talents and expects us to use them, to leverage and maximize them for his kingdom. Paul extolls us to do so throughout his gospels, and Christ teaches the very same in parables like those found in the middle part of Matthew 25. In Ephesians 2, in fact, Paul reminds us that we are "created in Christ Jesus to do good works, which God prepared in advance for us to do." Therefore, ability may not entirely be a gift, but it certainly isn't a curse either.

Yet God Redeems All Things

Our humanist tendencies (and even westernized Christianity) say that we are fine just as we are. That stands in direct contrast to the gospel message that we all need Jesus, and that all is still being made new—which reminds

---

1   Elyse Durham interviewed Bethany Sollereder about this theological concept in *Christianity Today* (15 July 2019): "Predators and Prey: Was death part of God's plan all along?"

us again that many things are wrong with this world.

I was created by God. As to whether he created me to be disabled (which gives value to my disability) or not (which can imply that he made a mistake or that he did not have some design for me as a disabled person), I know one thing for sure:

> *He created me to know him and to enjoy him—to find my life, my breath, and my being in him. In other words, my value is not wrapped up in any way in my disability. I am not more or less valuable as a person because of my disability. I am simply God's child.*

It is difficult to say this well, and yet it is so simple a thought. I happen to have a disability, and whether I have it from God's hand is not really as important as this: Does God have a purpose for my life? Can he use me despite my disability, or maybe even because of it? Can he reveal himself through my life? Can he use me to share his love, to extend his grace, to participate in his saving plan?

God redeems. From the moment of his first creative act up to today and every hour, he redeems.

And he uses me. He uses my disability. He uses my sins and my failings, and he redeems. He redeems me and others around me. He redeems them, also through me and my faltering speech.

He Redeems You

God may or may not have given me my disability, but

he definitely uses it. The same is true for you. Your value—whether or not you have a disability—is not determined by what you contribute, how independently you live, how impressive your resume looks, or whether you can feed yourself. Your value is complete because you are a child of the living God. Your value is hidden in him. And whether you are disabled, and whether or not that disability comes from God's hands, he still redeems.

I met my neighbor a long time ago when I was like eight years old, or maybe younger. We would go to each other through the fence and we would talk.

He and I bonded together so much that we were best friends. I still see him at my church, and we talk about everything. It's still like we are together at the fence and all that.

He would come over to my mom and dad's house and go swimming and play games. He's such a nice guy that he helps now with the Chicagoland Prison Outreach. He talks to inmates.

He's a caring guy, a very caring guy. He's disabled and he has a little speech problem. He's a very important guy to me, because he looks up to me and I look up to him and that's how we bond together, to each other.

He's just like a brother to me. It's just like a friendship that we have together. We still have. He's a wonderful person to me and means a lot to me.

Brett
Co-laborer
Elim Christian Services

Stage 4: Friendship

Think about your friends for a minute. What makes them your friends? Is it a common interest, shared experiences? Are you all fans of the same sports team, did you all go on a special trip together? Did you attend the same school or the same summer camp?

It's pretty safe to assume that we share some things in common with the people in our group of friends.

That "commonality" is the very thing that keeps us from becoming friends with people who are different from us. What would draw us to these people, after all? When we think of people with disabilities, we often think first of what makes us different: the disability. We talk about people with disabilities in these terms. We even call them "the disabled," "the blind," "the handicapped." Our language focuses first on the disability, and second on the person.

Why We Aren't Friends

But those aren't the only things that keep us from becoming friends with people who have disabilities. Here are some other impediments that keep us from becoming friends:

- **Different needs** – People who live with disabilities stand out for many reasons. They are different, and they have different needs. Whereas you can decide to get out of bed in the morning, a woman with cerebral palsy may need to be helped out of bed and into her wheelchair. She may need to be fed and transported to her job or her day program. She has different needs.

- **Different perspectives and priorities** – Life with a disability, by its very presence, forces one to live life with a different perspective, and even different priorities. When my friend Darrell experiences the assessment of others, it no longer bothers him. His perspective is that God knows who he is and loves him. And when we live with different perspectives, we also develop new priorities. Maybe our priorities become time with friends instead of time with the television. Maybe our priority is to meet new people instead of getting more work done. These perspectives and priorities are often so different from the norm, that we who live without disabilities can overlook the value of those different perspectives and priorities —we not only don't share those values, we don't even see them as valuable. The differences continue to keep us from relationship, from friendship.

- **Different lives** – Life with a disability is simply different. It is complicated and messy and medically-involved. It is never ever going to be fixed. This is frustrating for our friends without disabilities. They want us to be normal, they want to pray for our healing. And while our disabilities are not okay, or normal, they also are not the core problem. It is a different life, but it is not a lesser life. Yet, there still seems to be little common ground on which to build a friendship.

These differences understandably contribute to lives lived so differently that they are naturally lived apart from each other. We assume, for some reason, that this is as it should be.

Why Can't We be Friends?

These differences need not be the obstacles that we allow them to be. In fact, it is in some ways these very differences that ought to attract our attention and warrant our time.

Connecting with someone who lives with different needs can teach us both to be grateful for our own situation, and to be willing to assist with the needs of others: to be agents of God's mercy.

Developing an understanding of the different perspective and priorities of someone with disabilities can help us to see our own lives and God's world differently. It can give us a better sense of the presence of God's kingdom, and the upside-down-nature of the kingdom of this world. Seeing that someone who lives with disabilities would highly value just a few minutes of my time helps remind me that God wants me to spend time with him. It reminds me that I am not just what I do, or what I own, or what other people say about me: I am a beloved child of God and he just wants me.[2]

It is our differences that we allow to keep us from relationship with people who have disabilities. Yet it is in many ways those differences that have so much to teach us.

What might those perspectives and life experiences teach you?

What the Bible Says

I can give you many reasons to become friends, but the Scriptures call us to this kind of interdependent unity in so many ways already, that I'll let them do the talking.

Paul tells us in 1 Corinthians 11:33, "So then, my brothers and sisters, when you gather to eat, you should all eat together." And then Paul again in Ephesians 4:2–6 "Be completely humble and gentle; be patient, bearing with one another in love. Make every effort to keep the unity of the Spirit through the bond of peace. There is one body and one Spirit, just as you were called to one hope when you were called; one Lord, one faith, one baptism; one God and Father of all, who is over all and through all and in all." In 1 Corinthians 1:27–30, he writes, "But God chose the foolish things of the world to shame the wise; God chose the weak things of the world to shame the strong. God chose the lowly things of this world and the despised

---

2   See Henri Nouwen's *In the Name of the Jesus: Reflections on Christian leadership* (Chestnut Ridge NY: Crossroad Publishing, 1989) and *Life of the Beloved: Spiritual living in a secular world* (Chestnut Ridge NY: Crossroad Publishing, 1992).

things—and the things that are not—to nullify the things that are, so that no one may boast before him."

Now, having read these verses and having heard the Word of God, some of us are still reading these words and we are not convinced. "This is for someone else," your brain might be saying. "I am not built for this kind of thing."

That is exactly the point. You are not inclined to relationship with people who live with disabilities, and that is exactly why you need to develop one. Do you want to be part of building God's kingdom? Do you want his will to be done "on earth as it is in heaven?" Then reach out and invite a new person into your life.

How Do You Become Friends with Me?

Here are a few things you should do to prepare for those steps:

- Stop seeing the disability first. **Start seeing the person first.** Wouldn't it be wonderful if the lady in the wheelchair was just called Anne, instead?

- Stop being guarded and perfect. **Start being exposed and vulnerable.** None of us is who we appear to be. We are not the facades we put on for our fellow man. We are faltering, we are lonely, and we are hurting. While we grasp for perfection and stability and independence, we miss out on the healing touch of others, the peace of entrusting all things to God, and the true fellowship of life lived in interdependence and communion.

- Stop walking past people who are different. **Start**

being patient in your communications. Instead of a passing "Hi! How are you?" stop and introduce yourself and offer the opportunity to truly greet each other. You may even adopt this approach with your other friends.

• Stop assuming you know what life is like for people with disabilities. **Start asking questions.** If you want to become friends, you must get to know people. Just ask questions. Tell people about yourself, what you like and what is important to you, and find things you can talk about.

These are just a few tactics you can use to start developing a friendship with someone who lives with disabilities —not to mention, just about anyone else who lives a different kind of life. See the next chapter for more hands-on tips as you start down this road.

What does Friendship look like?

So, we know why we're not friends, and why we should become friends. But what does friendship actually look like?

I think, in many ways, we already know the answer.

It looks like an intentional relationship, built on more and more shared experiences. But a Christian friendship reflects something even more than that. This shared relationship is built on faith and is responsive to Christ's call to unity – that we are tied together by Christ alone and above all other things.

Friendship looks like this:

I have come to know and spend time with a friend who has a disability. This person has value in God's sight, but also in mine, and I know that my life is better for having known this person, and as much as I have helped her, she has also blessed me. In fact, I now like to initiate relationships with people who have disabilities. God brings many different people into my church and community, including people with disabilities, and we all benefit as we grow in friendship with each other.

Friendship means that we not only come alongside someone else, but that we begin to receive from that person as well. This is perhaps the most challenging reality to accept about relationships with people who are different: that they can help us, that they can assist in molding us into the people God calls us to be.

Friendship is mutual. It is reciprocal. A true friendship sees an exchange of gifts, of thoughts and opinions, of encouragement and chastisement, as an essential foundation. It is not friendship if it does not allow both parties to speak into the lives of the other. It is not friendship if it is only about what one can do for the other.

But most of all, we need to accept that we are the beloved children of God, and so are our brothers and sisters with disabilities. In our weaknesses, in our brokenness, in our gifts and talents, God reveals himself. To deny relationship with people who live with disabilities is to deny them the opportunity to use that which God has gifted to them, it is to deny ourselves the pleasure and blessing of that intimacy, and it is to ignore the commands of the apostle Paul and our Lord Jesus Christ.

What Steps Can I Take to Become Friends?

Reach out. Become a friend, and take another step toward reflecting God's kingdom, and his heart for unity, in your relationships.

Pray

- Ask God to reveal to you the giftedness of a person who lives with disabilities. Ask God for patience and insight to observe and value those gifts.
- Pray for a spirit of humility and servitude, that you might not see yourself more highly than you ought.

Reflect

- Why does it seem so overwhelming to think about becoming friends with someone who has a disability?
- What are the specific concerns I have about befriending someone who lives with disabilities? That they will demand too much of my time? That we will have nothing in common? That my life will change too much?
- Do I believe that this isn't for me? Why?
- Read 1 Corinthians 1:26–31. In it, Paul challenges the church in Corinth to recognize the "inverted" nature of the kingdom of God. The foolish are called

to shame the wise. The weak shame the strong. This is how God wants it to be in his church. How does your church allow God's strength to be made perfect in your weakness (2 Corinthians 12)? Is there room for God to speak through those the world sees as "foolish" or "weak"?

Act

- Encourage your church leadership to form a disability ministry team, if they do not already have one. Commit to serving on this team, and to enlisting fellow members. Consider focusing this team on creating a more welcoming and sensitive church environment. Focus less on creating new disability programs and more upon including people with disabilities in all aspects of your congregation's ministry.

- Talk with your family members and friends about the relationships they have with people who have disabilities. Ask them to share their thoughts on these friendships, and the challenges and joys of those relationships.

Questions to Consider

- o Why do we believe friends must be like us?
- o How does the Holy Spirit change that, especially in our churches?
- o Do you know anyone who has a friend with a disability? What caused them to become friends?

Resources

- If you really want to experience what friendship looks like, get connected with Friendship Ministries (friendship.org) and consider adding a Friendship class to your church's ministry programs. Or, if your congregation already has a Friendship class, volunteer as a teacher, a helper, or provide snacks or some other kind of assistance.

- When you become friends with people who have disabilities, you'll want to read the *Inclusion Handbook: Everybody belongs, everyone serves* (Reformed Church Press, 2013 [new edition forthcoming]), edited by Mark Stephenson and Terry A. De Young.

- Erik Carter's *Including People with Disabilities in Faith Communities: A guide for service providers, families, and congregations* (Baltimore MD: Paul H. Brookes Publishing, 2007 – ISBN 978-1557667434) provides a comprehensive and practical overview of the challenges of inclusion, as well as the importance of it.

- Two great resources for building an inclusive church are available from Joni and Friends at irresistiblechurch.org and from All Belong Center for Inclusive Education at allbelong.org..

My definition of a co-laborer is someone that works right alongside with me.

My job as a co-laborer is to just keep using my talents for the way God wants me to be.

God chooses others to use their talents in many ways. We all have different types of talents, but when they all come together for the glory of God, that's a great thing.

Treat people the way you want to be treated. Whenever I feel like treating a person the wrong way, I always remember that to be a co-laborer to someone means I need to be a co-laborer back.

Darrell
Co-laborer
Elim Christian Services

Stage 5: Co-Laborers

We all have certain friends who know our skills, gifts, and talents. They encourage us to develop, to reach for, and to achieve our goals and to not settle for less. They force us off our couches and into the world. They tell us we have something to contribute and they also tell us to make that contribution.

Friends like these are co-laborers. They don't coddle us, they don't put up with our excuses. They challenge us. They not only encourage us, they also confront us when we're wrong.

Who in your life does this for you? Conversely, to whom are you providing this kind of "co-laboring" friendship?

Co-laboring with People who have Disabilities

When we are approached by people with disabilities, we tend not to first imagine what they can do, but what they cannot do. We immediately absolve people with disabilities (and many other people who are different from us) from the work God has called each of us to. We unconsciously refuse to co-labor with people who have disabilities, all because of our unfair assumptions that actually *block people with disabilities from participating in God's kingdom work*.

Rather than first considering what people with disabilities cannot do, what if we instead thought first about what they *can do*? Let's be creative. Let's imagine what co-laboring with people who have disabilities can look like.

- **As a neighbor** – Imagine encouraging that family or that person a few doors down to answer God's call on their lives. Imagine having earned their trust and their friendship to the point where you can say, "I can see that John is an encourager. I have appreciated how he is always excited to see me. I wonder if you would be willing to let me spend some time with John occasionally and take him around the neighborhood. Maybe together, we can encourage the rest of our neighbors. Maybe we can bless them and provide the mercy of God in their lives."

- **At church** – Imagine talking to Casey, who sits in the row behind you at church, and finding out she has always wanted to work in daycare. Imagine going with her to find the nursery coordinator and figuring out how to get her included on the nursery schedule. Imagine finding out that Bill, who loves to sing at the top of his voice, has always wanted to sing with the choir. Your greatest chore now is not to work with Bill, but perhaps to work with the choir, to help them accept that God's will is not reflected in our perfection, but in our practice of his grace and in our enthusiasm in worship. Imagine enlisting Beverly to read the Scriptures, or Gene to be part of the deacon board. Imagine listening to our friends with disabilities, discerning their gifts and passions, and equipping them to answer God's call on their lives.

- **At work** – Shelly is loud, and yet she can barely speak. Her limbs seem to move constantly, yet she has so little control and so little strength, and she is in a wheelchair every time you see her. When you see her dad talk to her, his face is right in front of hers, and you have never, not even once, seen her respond, not with even so much as a hand signal or a nod of her head. What can Shelly do, really? How can she work? Imagine, for a moment, that you first found out from Shelly, as best you could, what she wanted. Imagine talking with her parents and loved ones and learning how to best communicate with Shelly. Maybe you would bring her to your business and enlist her to greet your coworkers and maybe a few customers each morning. Perhaps you would see something amazing happen. Perhaps you would re-define your understanding of what it really means to work. Maybe, as your coworkers and customers be-gan to greet Shelly on a daily basis, they would learn patience through their interactions with her. Maybe they would start to see that getting things done and moving on to the next thing is not the most im-portant thing. Maybe they would grow a heart for people who live with disabilities and feel less intim-idated about reaching out to others. Maybe work wouldn't be about making money for the business but be redefined as doing what God has called and equipped us to do, whatever that might be.

If we could follow through on this kind of imagining, in our neighborhoods, our churches, and in our workplaces, our lives could change dramatically.

One of the reasons this doesn't happen is because we can't imagine how this could possibly improve our lives and communities. But there are so many testimonies to the opposite. Here's how you can move beyond imagining to actually becoming a co-laborer:

Pray

- Pray for humility.
- Pray for strength to maintain a co-laboring attitude with those God has placed in your lives, family, friends, people with disabilities, neighbors, coworkers, and church members.
- Pray for patience when you do not get it right, when you take steps and fail, but, all the while, to keep making progress.

Reflect

- Read 1 Thessalonians 5:11 and Ephesians 2:10 and consider how these verses apply to each child of God.
- Do I generally divide the world into people who need help and people who give help to others?
- Why would I hire or not hire someone who has a disability to work for my company, or to be a co-worker?
- What challenges should our congregation address in

order to equip people with disabilities to be co-laborers in our community?

Act

- Begin advocating for the intentional inclusion of persons who live with disabilities into your business or workplace.
- Assist leaders in your congregation in finding people who live with disabilities, or their family members, to be part of leading ministries and programs in your church.

The highest expression of relationship is one in which each participant is encouraging, equipping, and challenging the other to become and achieve all they were created to be and do.

We have, for too long, believed that this was the domain of people who were like us, people who were capable, smart, uniquely gifted. In so doing, we overlook the people that we think of as incapable, inefficient, and unqualified.

But let's remember, God anointed the *youngest, (and later adulterous) shepherd son* of Jesse to be the king of his people. Earlier, he used a *fugitive, aged murderer who was afraid* to talk to lead his people out of Israel. He chose the *virgin bride of a carpenter* to bring his son into our world.

God uses who he chooses. When we co-labor, we not only give expression to this biblical truth, we become a living testimony for others to see.

Become a co-laborer and testify to God's power today and grace today.

Questions to Consider

- How have you encouraged your fellow co-laborers recently?
- In what ways does your congregation allow people with disabilities to participate in ministry, and in the work of the kingdom?

Resources

- Barb Newman and Betty Grit's *Accessible Gospel, Inclusive Worship* (ISBN 978-1530893003) provides practical insight and tools for including people with disabilities in all aspects of your congregation and its worship services.
- *Living Gently in a Violent World: The Prophetic Witness of Weakness* (Expanded edition: Downers Grove: IVP, 2018 – ISBN 978-0830834969), by Stanley Hauerwas and Jean Vanier, is a moving and deeply theological book that considers how Christians who include people with disabilities are prophesying to the world around them
- If you feel ready to teach *The 5 Stages* to others, you might enjoy our training video (www.the5stages.com/resources/presentations). You can even use the presentation resources we've provided to set up your own 5 Stages presentation (see "There is No Asterisk").

Conclusion

Our first instinct is to ignore people with disabilities, or perhaps to simply feel sorry for them. On rare occasions we may care for them, or we might even become friends.

But we almost never think of them as necessary, as essential, as partners in God's kingdom work.

That's because we put an asterisk on the Bible verses that call us to our work.

- From 2 Timothy 3:16 & 17: *"All Scripture is God-breathed and is useful for teaching, rebuking, correcting and training in righteousness, so that the servant of God may be thoroughly equipped for every good work."*

- 1 Thessalonians 5:11: *"Therefore encourage one another and build each other up, just as in fact you are doing."*

- Ephesians 2:10: *"For we are God's handiwork, created in Christ Jesus to do good works, which God prepared in advance for us to do."*

There is no asterisk on these verses—like an asterisk that would send your eyes to the bottom of the page, where you would see "except for people who have disabilities," or "except for people who are depressed," or "except for children who can't communicate well."

But even though there is no asterisk, we often subconsciously put an asterisk on these verses. Are we assuming that people who have disabilities are not called by God to do his work? Do we believe, even slightly, that people with different abilities are not supposed to be challenged, equipped, and encouraged for every good work, "which God has prepared in advance for them to do?"

We can't become co-laborers until we get rid of the asterisk. Are you putting an asterisk on these verses?

Are you absolving people with disabilities from the kingdom work of God?

Embrace Your Calling

God calls you to be a co-laborer. He did not call you just to be a disciple, but to make a disciple of others. That is your calling.

Are you going to answer? I've provided you with a ton of links and resources in this brief book to help you get started. And while ultimately, it is up to you, I also want to help.

If you want to get the guidance you need to become a co-laborer, you've already taken the first big step. Here's some options for your next step in the journey of disability attitudes:

- Find your nearest group home or disability services organization (Google can help). Reach out to them and find out what needs, both small and large, they might have. And find a way to interact with the individuals served there. These are your neighbors, and soon, they will be your co-laborers.

- Skim back through this booklet to find one resource that you will acquire and use to continue through your journey of disability attitudes.
- Share this book with others.

I am so thankful you've taken the time to read this book, and excited about the journey God is sending you to take. I want you to know you have help as you go through this journey. This book is a bit of a map for you, and you'll find plenty more resources and assistance along the way.

After all, this is what you are called to do. Go and do it. Become a co-laborer.

"As an educator deeply invested in inclusive education, and as a mother to an incredible autistic son, I have often wrestled with my own perceptions and attitudes about disability and how they can get in the way of loving my neighbor well, especially my disabled neighbor. Dan Vander Plaats has created a nuanced discussion of the different attitudes we may have about disability and provides multiple resources on how to move along the pendulum from ignorance, to pity, to caring, to friendship, and ultimately, to co-laboring, where we find ourselves in rich reciprocal relationships with disabled people that enables both of us to fulfill our God-given callings. Each step is inherent in our journey and his booklet provides all the support we need to take the first step. Whether you are a teacher, pastor, church member or parent, I highly recommend this booklet as you consider how you view disability and how that impacts your relationships with the disabled. Let's make our communities inclusive places where abled and disabled people can walk out the path God has placed before them, hand in hand."

Sarah Ternes, Stateside Educational Consultant,
Missionary Ventures International (MVI.org)

"Dan's message of love towards people with disabilities and including them in the church has transformed many lives. I greatly admire him."

Daryl Garcia, Church Outreach Coordinator,
Tesoros de Dios (tesorosdedios.org)